**What is... ?**

# Squasny

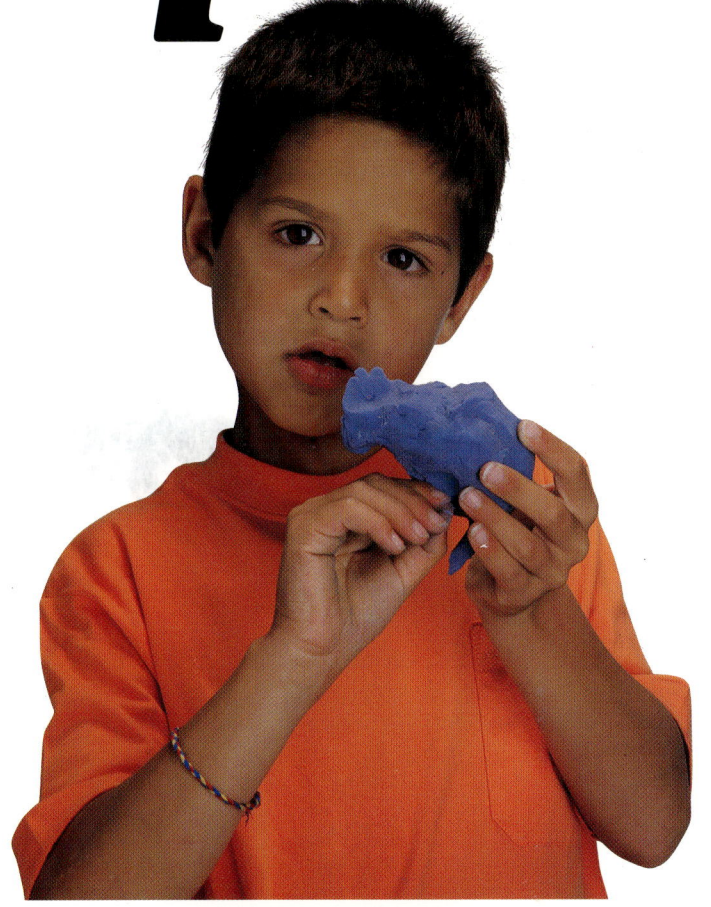

Heinemann

First published in Great Britain by Heinemann Library
an imprint of Heinemann Publishers (Oxford) Ltd
Halley Court, Jordan Hill, Oxford OX2 8EJ

MADRID ATHENS PARIS
FLORENCE PRAGUE WARSAW
PORTSMOUTH NH CHICAGO SAO PAULO
SINGAPORE TOKYO MELBOURNE AUCKLAND
IBADAN GABORONE JOHANNESBURG

© Heinemann Publishers (Oxford) Ltd

Designed by Heinemann Publishers (Oxford) Ltd
Printed in China

99 98 97 96 95
10 9 8 7 6 5 4 3 2 1

ISBN 0431 07978 1

**British Library Cataloguing in**
Warbrick, Sar.
Squashy. - (What is...? Series,
I. Series
500

Acknowledgements
The Publishers would like to thank the following
for the kind loan of equipment and materials used in
this book: Comet, Harlow; Early Learning Centre, Bishop Stortford;
Malsens, Bishop Stortford; Salisbury's, Harlow.
Toys supplied by Toys Я Us Ltd,
the world's biggest toy megastore.

Special thanks to Anna, Bryan, Doris and Mina, George, Kevin, Leigh,
Michael and Nadia who appear in the photographs

Photographs: Chris Honeywell pp2(r), 3(l), 4, 14, 15;
other photographs by Trevor Clifford
Commissioned photography arranged by Hilary Fletcher
Cover Photography: Chris Honeywell

There are squashy things all around us.
Squashy things can be fun.
Squashy things can be useful.
Squashy things can also be messy!

This book shows you what is squashy.

These objects look different.
What differences can you see?

In one way they are all the same.
They are squashy.

When Anna squashes a pillow, she pushes air out.

Hug a teddy bear and see what happens.

How would you make all these clothes fit in the suitcase?

Kevin has squashed all the air out!

What happens when you squash a balloon?

Suddenly, all the air comes out with a big bang!

**What happens when George squashes a wet sponge?**

He can wash his toy car.

When Michael squashes an orange . . .

he can drink the juice.

Clay can be squashed.

Leigh is making a model.

15

The icing is being squashed through the nozzle to decorate the cake.

Look at the different shapes it makes.

These balls aren't squashy by themselves.

But put a lot of them together and look how squashy they are!

What is squashy here?

21

# Index

air 4, 7, 9
balloons 8, 9
balls 18, 19
bananas 2, 3
bean bag 2, 3
clay 14, 15
clothes 6, 7
icing 16, 17
juice 13
orange 12, 13
pillow 4
sponge 10, 11
teddy bear 5